Babe
DIDRIKSON
ZAHARIAS

BABE DIDRIKSON ZAHARIAS

by Mackenzie Lobby

ABDO
Publishing Company

Content Consultant: Karen Bednarski
president, The GolfSource

Published by ABDO Publishing Company, 8000 West 78th Street, Edina, Minnesota 55439. Copyright © 2011 by Abdo Consulting Group, Inc. International copyrights reserved in all countries. No part of this book may be reproduced in any form without written permission from the publisher. SportsZone™ is a trademark and logo of ABDO Publishing Company.

Printed in the United States of America,
North Mankato, Minnesota
112010
012011

 THIS BOOK CONTAINS AT LEAST 10% RECYCLED MATERIALS.

Editor: Paula Lewis
Copy Editor: David Johnstone
Series Design: Christa Schneider
Cover Production: Christa Schneider
Interior Production: Sarah Carlson and Christa Schneider

Library of Congress Cataloging-in-Publication Data
Lobby, Mackenzie, 1982-
  Babe Didrikson Zaharias : groundbreaking all-around athlete / by Mackenzie Lobby.
    p. cm. — (Legendary athletes.)
  Includes bibliographical references and index.
  ISBN 978-1-61714-755-5
  1. Zaharias, Babe Didrikson, 1911-1956—Juvenile literature. 2. Athletes—United States—Biography—Juvenile literature. 3. Women athletes—United States—Biography—Juvenile literature. I. Title.
  GV697.Z26L63 2011
  796.0922—dc22
  [B]
                        2010041158

TABLE OF CONTENTS

CHAPTER 1

Babe Didrikson was a one-woman team at the 1932
AAU National Championships.

A One-Woman Show

Thousands of track and field fans filled the grandstands of Dyche Stadium in Evanston, Illinois, on July 16, 1932. They came to view an important track meet: the women's American Athletic Union (AAU) National Championships. The event also served as the Olympic Trials for those who hoped to make the 1932 US Olympic team. During the opening ceremonies, each team marched into the stadium.

Most teams consisted of 15 to 20 women who were dressed in matching uniforms. Then there was Babe—a one-woman team. The announcer's voice boomed over the loudspeaker, "Mildred 'Babe' Didrikson, representing the Employers Casualty Company of Dallas, Texas."[1] On cue, the 21-year-old Didrikson proudly ran onto the field by herself and waved her arms. The stadium erupted as many people rose to their feet and cheered for this young athlete. She was there to win—not just one event, but the entire meet single-handedly.

A Day of Competition

Didrikson's coach, Colonel Melvin Jackson McCombs, was the manager of women's sports teams for Employers Casualty Company, an insurance firm in Dallas. He had recruited Didrikson to be a part of the company-sponsored women's team, the Golden Cyclones. The team competed in softball, basketball, and track and field events.

Based on his research of the AAU National Championships and Olympic Trials competitors, he stated, "I think . . . you can do something that's never been done before. I believe . . . you can win the national championship for us all by yourself."[2] With no teammates to rely on, Babe Didrikson left her home in Texas and headed to Evanston, Illinois, in hopes of earning her ticket to the Olympic Games.

More than 200 women competed in the 1932 US Olympic Trials meet. Most teams had at least 15 athletes;

Extreme Athletes

Today, a female athlete such as Babe Didrikson would have the opportunity to enter the heptathlon. The heptathlon requires one athlete to compete in seven events over two days for a single score. On the first day, a heptathlete competes in the 100-meter hurdles, high jump, shot put, and 200-meter run. The second day of competition includes long jump, javelin, and the 800-meter run.

Prior to the introduction of the heptathlon in 1981, some athletes competed in the pentathlon, which consisted of five events. While women currently compete in the heptathlon, the men compete in the decathlon, which includes ten events.

the Illinois Women's Athletic Club was the largest team with 22 members. Didrikson, as the only member of the Golden Cyclones team, entered eight of the ten events at the meet: shot put, javelin throw, broad jump, baseball throw, 80-meter hurdles, high jump, discus, and 100-meter dash.

It was a busy day for Didrikson. As soon as she completed her first heat in the 80-meter hurdles, she squeezed in an attempt at the high jump. Afterward, she hurried over to compete in the broad jump, the shot put, and the javelin. She managed to run the 100-meter dash and take her turn at the discus and baseball throw as well. Most of the other athletes competed only in two or three events and had ample time between each event. At times, the judges held up heats and finals as Didrikson competed in another event or needed to rest between events. Still, she performed better than most of her competitors.

Track Measurements

Measurements in track and field traditionally are in the metric system, which is based on meters. However, in the early part of the twentieth century, running events in the United States used the Imperial system, which uses feet and yards. One yard is three feet—approximately .91 meters. While international competitions such as the Olympics still used the 100-, 200-, and 400-meter dashes, some meets in the United States used the 100-, 220-, and 440-yard dashes. As of 1976, US track meets use metric measurements.

Despite the lack of rest, Didrikson won five events: shot put, javelin, broad jump, baseball throw, and 80-meter hurdles. The high jump was her last event. As the overall points were tallied and the last jumps were taken, the crowd waited in anxious anticipation. With only Babe Didrikson and Jean Shiley of Philadelphia remaining, the high jump bar was raised just over the world-record height: 5 feet 3 3/16 inches (1.6 m). First, Shiley cleared the height. Didrikson soared over the bar as well. When it was moved up, neither succeeded, leading to a tie for first place between the two women—along with a new world record.

The crowd celebrated as the scores were announced. The 22-member Illinois Women's Athletic Club finished with 22 points. Didrikson, a one-woman team, earned 30 points, making her a national champion, the overall team title winner for the Golden Cyclones, and a 1932 Olympic qualifier. After her victory, she roamed the field and greeted her new fans. They would watch her closely as she competed against the best in the world at the Olympics in Los Angeles several weeks later.

George Kirksey, a United Press reporter, said that Didrikson's feat was "the most amazing series of performances ever accomplished by any individual, male or female, in track and field history."[3]

A Lifelong Athlete

While Didrikson gained fame in track and field, her athletic prowess reached much further. After her Olympic debut in 1932, she displayed her athletic talents by competing in billiards, bowling, basketball, baseball, and tennis. Reporters and fans called her the "wonder girl."[4] But her athletic encore and most crowning moments occurred on the golf course. It was there that she found herself and her life's passion.

The path Didrikson took to achieve greatness in athletics, however, was not always smooth. It was a long and sometimes painful journey that highlighted

A Record-Breaking Day

Not only did Didrikson win the overall 1932 AAU National Championship and the US Olympic Trials meet, she also broke three of her own world records that day. She threw the baseball 272 feet, 2 inches (82.96 m) and the javelin 139 feet, 3 inches (42.44 m). She ran her first heat in the 80-meter hurdles in 11.9 seconds, winning the final heat in 12.1 seconds. She and Jean Shiley tied for first place in the high jump by setting a new world record. Didrikson also won the shot put and set a US record with a throw of 39 feet 6 1/4 inches (12.05 m). She won the broad jump with 17 feet 6 inches (5.33 m). She came in fourth in discus. The 100-meter dash was the only event in which she did not qualify.

Regarding her win of the AAU National Championship and the Olympic Trials meet, Didrikson said, "It was just one of those days in an athlete's life when you know you're just right. You feel you could fly."[5]

Olympic Hopefuls

In track and field, a US national championship meet is held each year. Every four years, that meet also serves as the US Olympic Trials for the Summer Olympics. These Olympic Trials are the tryouts for athletes who hope to make the US Olympic team.

her inner strength and resolve. Babe Didrikson, the "wonder girl," blazed trails in women's sports and earned trophies like no other athlete had ever done. Her long list of triumphs, and the barriers she had to overcome to achieve them, made her what many people consider the greatest female athlete of all time.

Didrikson practiced jumping hurdles at Dyche Stadium.

CHAPTER 2

Babe, *left*, with her brother Arthur and her sister Lillie

Growing Up in Texas

Babe's father, Ole Nickolene Didriksen Sr., emigrated from Norway to Port Arthur, Texas, in 1905, leaving behind his wife, Hannah Marie, and three children, Ole, Dora, and Esther. A carpenter, Ole Sr. built a home in Texas and worked for three years before saving enough money to send for his family in 1908.

In 1909, Hannah gave birth to twins, Lillie and Louis. Babe was born Mildred Ella Didriksen on June 26, 1911, in Port Arthur, Texas. In her autobiography, she claims to have been born in 1914. On her application for the 1932 Olympics, she stated it was 1913, and she listed 1919 when applying for a visa. A baptismal certificate held by her sister, Lillie, however, lists 1911 as Babe's birth year, and this has become the widely accepted year of her birth. In 1915, Arthur was born.

In that year, a major hurricane struck Port Arthur and the Didriksen home. The family lost many of their belongings in their flooded home.

What's in a Name?

When Mildred Ella was the baby of the family, her mother called her Baden, which is Norwegian for baby. Some historians say the English version, baby, was shortened to Babe when her younger brother was born. Others say she often said that she was nicknamed Babe for her batting ability after the famous baseball player Babe Ruth. In either case, the nickname Babe continued.

The spelling of Babe's maiden name has been a point of confusion as well since her given name was Didriksen. Once misspelled as Didrikson in her elementary school records, Babe chose to use the new spelling, saying, "I wanted everyone to know I was a Norwegian, not a Swede."[1] Despite her intentions, the "sen" version is actually more common in Norway.

Rather than rebuild, the family moved to the shipping port of Beaumont, Texas, for a new start and bought a home on Doucette Avenue. The trolley line that ran down the center of their street, coupled with a houseful of energetic children, made for a chaotic, noisy, and happy upbringing.

Amidst financial struggles, Ole and Hannah provided a loving, supportive home. With the children gathered around him, Ole made up stories. Music often filled the house. Babe played the harmonica, bought with money she earned from mowing lawns. Her siblings and father played the piano or the violin while her mother sang. Some evenings, the entire neighborhood would come out on their porches and listen to the musical renderings of the Didriksen family orchestra.

Babe roller-skating in the neighborhood

A Troublemaker

Babe's determination and competitive spirit made her an exceptional young athlete. While attending Magnolia Elementary School in Beaumont, she once was caught climbing to the top of the school's flagpole. She was known to recruit the neighborhood children in her mischief as well, earning her the nickname "the Worst Kid on Doucette."[2]

Babe just could not seem to behave herself. One day, after picking up ground beef at the store for her mother, she was distracted by a neighborhood baseball game on the way home. Babe remembered,

Making Ends Meet

The Didriksens often struggled to make ends meet. All of the Didriksen children found jobs. In addition to mowing lawns, Babe worked at a local grocery store and in a fig-packing plant. At the plant, she had the tedious job of peeling rotten spots off the figs and washing the fruit. At one point, she took a part-time position at a factory sewing shut burlap sacks full of potatoes. Although she only made one cent per bag, she could sew quickly, so she earned a good income.

Babe's work did not end at the factory, however. When she and her siblings were not at school, working, or playing, they pitched in at home to help their mother. The big house on Doucette Avenue required a lot of work to keep it clean. One of Babe's chores was to wash the floor. Although her mother insisted that she get down on her hands and knees to scrub, Babe found it more efficient and fun to "skate" the floor clean by affixing the scrub brushes to her feet.

"I laid the package of meat down on the ground. I was only going to play for a couple of minutes, but they stretched into an hour."[3] When her mother showed up at the baseball field and discovered Babe playing baseball (the meat had been consumed by a neighborhood dog), she chased her daughter all the way home. Babe's brother Ole Jr. said, "She was just too active to settle down. She always wanted to be running, jumping, or throwing."[4] Lucky for her, she eventually found an outlet for her need to be constantly active.

A Budding Athlete

Lillie, one of Babe's older sisters and best friends, remembered Babe during her younger years, noting, "She was the best at everything we did."[5] Whether she hurdled over hedges or played marbles, Babe was an athlete. In elementary school, she ran up and down Doucette Avenue, hurdling the neighbors' hedges one after the next. However, one hedge was too high for her to jump over. Her solution was to talk to the neighbor, who then trimmed the hedge to her desired height. To avoid being scratched while jumping over the wide hedges, Babe bent her knee—a style she kept even when jumping over the narrow hurdles in track events. When she was not running and hurdling through her neighbors' yards, she played sandlot baseball and hit many home runs.

Eligibility

While Babe excelled at sports, she was not as notable in the classroom. Although she never failed a course, Babe seemed to do the bare minimum in order to pass at least three courses to remain eligible to participate on the school sports teams.

Once she entered David Crockett Junior High School, Babe became widely recognized for her athletic abilities. Ruby Gage, the teacher in charge of physical education and playground activities, said, "[Babe] could master any sport she wanted to. Marbles— anything—you name it and she could do it better than anybody else."[6]

Babe's early experience with competition, whether it was on Doucette Avenue or the junior high athletic fields, set the stage for a history-making career in athletics that no one in Beaumont, other than Babe, would have dreamed possible. "Before I was ever in my teens, I knew exactly what I wanted to be when I grew up. My goal was to be the greatest athlete that ever lived."[7]

Babe's parents, Hannah and Ole

CHAPTER 3

Babe practiced her football kicking form.

National Recognition

Many admired Babe for her athletic skills, but some of her junior high classmates thought she was too rough. Still drawn to the sandlot rather than the more typical girl activities, her strength and competitive spirit were unusual and intimidating.

When she entered Beaumont High School, the football team's star halfback, "Red" Reynolds, approached Babe. He was aware of her reputation and wanted to assert his dominance by challenging Babe to a boxing match. Never one to shy away from competition, she accepted. Reynolds teased her, "Hit me as hard as you can, you can't hurt me."[1] But one punch from Babe put Reynolds down on the ground. Later in life, he bragged about being knocked out by the famous Babe.

A Basketball Star Is Born

Babe's athletic talent was best displayed on Beaumont High School's organized sports teams, rather than boxing in the gym or the school

Babe and Jackie Bridgewater played on the Beaumont High School girls' basketball team, the Royal Purples.

hallways. In addition to playing on every girls' team in high school, Babe nearly had the opportunity to be the kicker on the boys' football team. The coach spent time training her, but Texas league rules prohibited girls from participating in boys' sports.

Earning a spot on the girls' basketball team, the Royal Purples, was Babe's biggest challenge. After being told she was too small in her freshman year, she worked on her shooting, dribbling, and passing skills. She even recruited the boys' basketball coach to give her training advice. She finally won a spot on the girls' varsity team in her junior year. The practice paid off.

Babe led the team in scoring from her first game. By the end of the season, she was named to the all-city and all-state basketball teams.

In 1930, Babe's career in athletics became a reality. Colonel Melvin Jackson McCombs sat in the stands at a Royal Purples game in Houston, Texas, and took notice of Babe's talent. The manager of a women's athletic program sponsored by the Employers Casualty Company, McCombs was in the right place at the right time. He watched as Babe scored 26 points that game, leading her team to a state championship. He knew he had to recruit her to play for his company team.

Golden Cyclones Basketball

In the 1930s, women's amateur basketball quickly

Sports and Society

When Babe was born, women did not have the right to vote or hold public office. They did not share the same rights as men and were considered second-class citizens. Married women were not encouraged to work outside the home as it would "take away" from their roles as a wife or mother. Women, single or married, could not hold political offices and were not welcome in competitive sports. Not only deemed unladylike, athletics were thought to diminish a woman's capability for childbearing.

Babe was nine years old on August 26, 1920, when the Nineteenth Amendment to the US Constitution became law. This granted women the right to vote. That was also the year in which the United States sent its first women's team to the Olympics. Despite the amendment, much of society considered women's participation in sports to be improper. Babe's dedication and participation in sports broke many social barriers and paved the way for other athletes.

became a popular spectator sport. Various organizations around the country, from corporations to churches, fielded teams. McCombs invited Babe to take a clerical job with Employers Casualty in 1930 and play for his championship team, the Golden Cyclones. With her parents' blessings and a special arrangement with the principal, which allowed her to return to school at the end of the school year to take her final exams and graduate from high school, Babe was off to Dallas, Texas.

Working and Competing

In addition to playing basketball, Colonel McCombs hired Babe to work as a typist at Employers Casualty Company, paying her $75 per month. In the midst of the Great Depression, this was a lofty sum. Babe paid $20 for room and board, sent $45 home each month, and saved $10.

Most of Babe's teammates enjoyed a similar arrangement. The Golden Cyclones were some of the most talented female athletes in the nation. Many were hired not for their skills at the typewriter but for their skills on the basketball court. The company had a mission of creating winning teams to promote the company. McCombs took care to ensure that the athletes were comfortable and not tempted to be lured away by other teams. The women were provided with uniforms, cutting-edge athletic equipment, and top-notch coaching.

During the 1931 basketball season, some of Babe's teammates expressed their distaste for her brashness and boasting. While this behavior was expected in male athletes, it was not accepted in women athletes. Her teammates felt she was no longer a team player and that success had inflated her ego and made her more demanding. In addition, her salary had increased to $1,080 ($90 per month), significantly more than what most of the other members of the team made.

Babe made her Golden Cyclones debut on the court the same day she arrived in Dallas. The team played the Sun Oil Company team, whose players were well aware of Babe's growing celebrity and hoped to win big to prove their superiority. Instead, Babe led her team to a 48–18 win, scoring 14 points. The team gained steam from that game, and Babe continued to star. By winter, the Golden Cyclones played in the AAU National Championships in Wichita, Kansas. Although they lost the championship game by a single point to the Sun Oil Company, Babe was named an All-American forward.

Golden Cyclones Track Season

With the success of the Golden Cyclones basketball team, Colonel McCombs decided to start a track team in 1930. Babe was immediately drawn to the new challenge—although she had never seen a track meet before. Under McCombs's tutelage, Babe diligently practiced the various events. In May 1930, she entered her first track and field meet at Southern Methodist University. She continued to enter a series of track meets that summer. She won every event in which she competed—the broad jump, high jump, 440-yard dash, and 100-yard dash. Babe was unstoppable.

By the end of the season, Babe owned southern AAU records in the high jump, broad jump, and eight-pound shot put. She also held national AAU records in the baseball throw and javelin. As a team, the Golden Cyclones finished second in the AAU National Championship track and field meet that year.

No Off-Season for Babe

Babe then moved on to represent the Golden Cyclones in softball, tennis, and springboard and platform diving. Once the 1931 basketball season began, she was eager to put together a winning season. With Babe as their star forward, the Golden Cyclones won the AAU National Championship. Averaging 33 points each game that season, Babe was again selected as an All-American.

During the 1931 track season, Babe set records in the broad jump, baseball throw, and 80-meter hurdles. Scoring 15 of the team's 19 points at the AAU National Championship meet, Babe caught the eye of the media. The *Dallas Morning News* called Babe "the world's outstanding all round feminine athlete."[2]

In the 1932 basketball season, Babe was named an All-American athlete for the third consecutive year. That year, she also took the AAU National Championships/Olympic Trials track meet by storm. Earning a place on the US Olympic team was a crowning achievement. Two years earlier, Babe had played sandlot baseball. Now the headlines proclaimed her to be the world's best female athlete.

Babe was a diver on the Golden Cyclones team.

CHAPTER 4

Didrikson practiced the javelin throw.

The 1932 Olympics

O n July 18, 1932, Babe Didrikson and the women's track and field team boarded a train in Chicago to travel to Los Angeles. With a US Olympic team sign on the side of the train, the young women felt like celebrities in a time when such a train trip was a luxury. Of the trip, Didrikson said,

> Most of the girls sat around watching the scenery and playing cards and gabbing. I was busy taking exercises and doing my hurdle bends and stuff. I'd practice in the aisle. Several times a day I'd jog the whole length of the train and back. People in the other cars took to calling out, "Here she comes again!"[1]

Just two weeks after winning the 1932 US Olympic Trials in track and field, Didrikson marched into the Olympic Stadium before 100,000 cheering fans. The team members wore white skirts and blouses, red vests, and white shoes provided by the Olympic Committee. "I couldn't enjoy the ceremonies that much . . . that was about

Quick Statistics

The first Olympic Games in which women competed were held in Paris, France, in 1900. The women represented the United States, France, Great Britain, Switzerland, and Bohemia.

In 1920, the United States entered its first women's team (swimmers) in the Olympics.

Women's track and field events were not a part of the Olympics until 1928, eight years after the Nineteenth Amendment became law.

The Olympic Games in 1932 occurred at a time when the nation was experiencing the Great Depression. The games were reduced to 16 days.

Of the 1,332 Olympic athletes in 1932, only 10 percent were female. An unprecedented 105,000 spectators filled the Los Angeles Coliseum, and 50,000 sports fans waited outside the stadium.

the first time I'd ever worn a pair of stockings in my life," she later acknowledged. "I was used to anklets and socks. And as for those shoes, they were really hurting my feet."[2] But on that July day, she waited patiently in the hot California sun with her American teammates—ready to make her dreams a reality.

In 1932, there were only five individual women's Olympic events in track and field. Each athlete was restricted to competing in no more than three events. Didrikson decided to enter in her strongest events: the javelin, the 80-meter hurdles, and the high jump.

Throwing for Gold

Her first event was the javelin competition, which was the first time women competed in that event. Since the infield was full of other athletes, Didrikson was unable to go through her usual warm-up by taking several practice throws. The scorching morning sun turned into cool shadows on the infield, causing her muscles to become tight and cold. Didrikson focused on the flag planted in the ground and waving in the distance. It signified the world record that had been set by Didrikson two weeks earlier in the US Olympic Trials.

With the spear poised, she slowly pulled back her body, fired forward, and watched as the javelin rocketed beyond the flag. Her throw of 143 feet, 4 inches (43.69 m) created an Olympic record and a world record. During that powerful throw, she tore cartilage in her shoulder; her next two attempts were not as successful. Luckily, it did not matter. Her first spectacular throw was enough to win a gold medal in the event and set the first Olympic record in the event.

A Second Win

After two days of rest, Didrikson returned to the stadium for the 80-meter hurdles. To make it to the final race, she had to do well in her qualifying heat. A favorite in the event, she crossed the finish in 11.8 seconds. In the qualifying round, she broke both the Olympic and world records.

The following day was the final race. Filled with nervous energy, Didrikson took off before the gun fired. The official called everyone back to the starting

False Start

False starts are common in track and field. In the excitement of the moment, a runner may anticipate the sound of the starting gun, rather than reacting to it, causing an early start. In running events, each competitor is allowed one false start. Upon a second false start, the athlete is disqualified.

line. She had to be careful— two false starts disqualified a runner from competition. The second time, Babe was careful to not jump the gun. The runners got off to a fair start. As they barreled down the straightaway, Evelyne Hall of Chicago, Illinois, took the lead. By the last two hurdles, Hall and Didrikson were even and appeared to reach the finish simultaneously. Didrikson threw her arms up in victory and exclaimed that she had won. But the Olympic timer said both women reached the tape in 11.7 seconds. After nearly 30 minutes of discussion, the judges announced that Didrikson won the event and her second gold medal.

The Final Event

Didrikson's last event of the 1932 Olympic Games was the high jump. She hoped to complete her gold medal sweep by winning the event. Just as in the US Olympic Trials, Didrikson and Shiley were the final women after multiple jumps. Each had cleared 5 feet 5 1/4 inches (1.66 m)—approximately 2 inches (5 cm) higher than the world record set at the US Olympic Trials. The bar was raised. Both women made their

Didrikson, *second from the right*, beat her teammate, Evelyne Hall, *right*, over the last hurdle to win the women's 80-meter hurdles in the 1932 Olympics.

final jumps. The crowd was riveted by the two US rivals who had jumped higher than any woman had before.

When the judges stepped in, Didrikson's dream of three gold medals was about to be lost. Her "Western roll" approach to the high jump was unusual to the judges, who ruled that her last jump did not count because she had gone headfirst, instead of feetfirst, over the bar. Along with many of her fans, she felt that the judges were wrong and simply did not understand her unorthodox method of jumping. After all, she had used the same technique throughout the competition.

Although she was disappointed, she accepted the silver medal with gratitude. Didrikson left the 1932 Olympic Games with three medals and two world records.

Arriving in Dallas, she was greeted by a crowd of fans. Wearing a sailor cap and an Olympic shirt, she stepped off the airplane, taking the massive public attention in stride. When approached by a reporter for comment, Didrikson said, "I made eight world's records in the last month and I am terribly happy."[3]

Disqualification

Didrikson's supporters challenged the judges' ruling that had disqualified her last high jump. One reporter, Frank G. Menke, wrote, "She twice shattered the world's record for the high jump and then was deprived of the high jump honors by two weird rulings by officials."[4]

Didrikson also questioned the ruling:

> I jumped in all parts of the United States before some of the best judges in the country and they all approved that method and even the judges out there Sunday afternoon [at the Olympics] had nothing to say about it until I had

twice cleanly cleared the bar.[5]

The winner, Jean Shiley, agreed with the judges and contested that Didrikson had been fouling her jumps all along. But she had decided to let it play out in competition.

Didrikson's "Western roll" was one of many techniques used by high jumpers in the early days when they had to land in sand pits or ground-level matting. By landing on their feet, they were less likely to be injured. Modern high jumping mats are set higher so the athletes can land on their backs.

Didrikson broke the high jump record but was disqualified for going headfirst over the bar.

CHAPTER 5

After the Olympics, Didrikson was back at work at Employers Casualty.

An Unwelcome Scandal

Babe Didrikson's performance at the 1932 Olympics earned her celebrity status. She was the obvious choice to receive the Female Athlete of the Year award in 1932, which was determined by the Associated Press poll of sports editors. They wrote, "Babe Breaks Records Easier Than Dishes."[1] Once the lavish homecoming after the Olympics was over, and the excitement waned, Didrikson still needed to make a living. She returned to her job at Employers Casualty Company doing clerical work for $300 per month.

With a steady income and a bright future, Didrikson decided to make the first big purchase of her adult life: a red Dodge coupe. To her surprise, her image, along with a photo of the car she had bought, appeared in a Dodge advertisement several weeks later. This spurred a scandal between Didrikson and the AAU. Since the AAU assumed she had received compensation for appearing in the advertisement, they stripped her of her status as an amateur athlete. Didrikson

Paving the Way

Didrikson helped pave the way for women's sports in the United States. In the three Olympics during the first decade of the twentieth century, some women appeared only in exhibition events such as archery, golf, yachting, and croquet. In the 1920s and 1930s, many doctors advised women and girls against participating in athletics, fearing that it was too stressful and would harm their reproductive systems. Although women were allowed to compete in Olympic swimming events beginning in 1912, it was not until standout performances, such as Didrikson's in 1932, that women's sports entered the mainstream.

angrily contested the matter, asserting that she had never given Dodge permission to use her likeness and that she had not been compensated. E. Gordon Perry of Dodge confirmed her story. Multiple telegrams between Didrikson and the AAU eventually settled the matter, allowing her amateur status to be reinstated.

After the issue with the AAU, Didrikson proceeded with caution regarding her athletic career. The advantage to remaining an amateur was the greater number of competitive opportunities. However, turning professional would give Didrikson more financial freedom. After receiving no apology from the AAU, she thought about what other options were available to her. She decided to take advantage of her current fame by turning professional, giving her the chance to sign endorsement deals and make significantly more money.

On the Road

In a twist of irony, Didrikson's first endorsement was for Dodge. Represented by her new agent, George P. Emerson, the company sought to compensate Didrikson for the trouble they had caused with the coupe advertisement.

Following an appearance for Dodge, she was booked to star in her own vaudeville show. The 18-minute theatrical performance included a series of peculiar routines. She started by singing, then displayed her athletic talent running on a treadmill, jumping a hurdle, and hitting plastic golf balls. The show concluded with her playing several songs on her harmonica. The crowds loved her. Performing four or five shows a day with the potential to make $2,500 per week, Didrikson had the opportunity to bank more money than she ever could have imagined. However, a life in vaudeville meant spending all of her time on stage or on the road. After one week, she decided to cancel future bookings.

So began a period in Didrikson's life marked by a string of seemingly random employment opportunities and endorsements. She was no longer able to engage in amateur athletics. With few opportunities to make

Didrikson and Ruth McGinnis competed in a billiards match.

a living in women's professional sports, Didrikson
sought out other ways to display her talents. Following
her vaudeville stint, she traveled to New York to
play in one women's basketball game and then in an
exhibition billiards game against the nation's best,
Ruth McGinnis.

A New Sport for Babe

Although she was not quite sure what she was
looking for, Didrikson had not found her niche in life.

The constant traveling and lack of routine became tiresome. She had saved enough money to forgo employment for a period of time and decided to invest herself seriously in golf—a game she had not played since high school. Didrikson did not plan on simply learning a skill. She planned on rising to the top of the game.

Upon moving to Los Angeles, she visited a golf club to acquaint herself with the local professionals. After watching golf pro Stan Kertes hit golf balls at an exhibition driving range event, she approached him. "She came up to me and said, 'Gee, you swing nice. Can you teach me that?' I knew her, of course, from the Olympics, and I said, 'Sure, we'll start now,'" explained Kertes.[2]

This was the beginning of Didrikson's training in the game of golf. From morning until night, she was at the golf course hitting balls, practicing putts, and learning from Kertes. He once said of her,

> She hit ball after ball until her hands began to bleed, and I had to make her wear gloves and finally beg her to stop and rest . . . I knew she had the makings of a champion.[3]

Playing Billiards

Ruth McGinnis, known as a billiards pioneer, grew up in her father's pool hall in Pennsylvania. By the age of seven, she was mentioned in the local press as a rising star on the billiards scene. The highly publicized game with Didrikson highlighted McGinnis's dominance in the sport as she devastated her opponent with a score of 400 to 62.

After spending six months focused solely on her training, hitting more than 1,000 balls a day, Didrikson moved back to Texas and began working at Employers Casualty again.

Shortly thereafter, she signed with an exhibition basketball team called "Babe Didrikson's All Americans." Comprised of four men and three women, the barnstorming All Americans traveled around the country entertaining crowds. They traveled to many rural towns for games and spent countless hours on the road. Although Didrikson was once again traveling for a living, golf stayed at the forefront of her mind. She knew she had a future in the game, and she had not given up on that dream.

After the basketball season ended in 1934, Didrikson went to Florida to pitch several spring training baseball games. She then pitched for an all-male

Basketball

Didrikson made $1,000 each month as part of Babe Didrikson's All Americans basketball team. The team played a total of 91 games, traveling in a seven-passenger sedan. While this was not the star treatment Didrikson had received in the past, she was also supporting her parents and helping out her siblings. The compensation was too attractive to pass up.

baseball team, the House of David. Her athletic ability attracted fans, but she only pitched the first inning. Then she would take off on her own and drive to the city that was scheduled for the next appearance of the House of David. She benefited financially, earning as much as $1,500 a month, but as her friend Ruth Scurlock explained, "[It] was terribly hard on her, physically and emotionally, but spiritually, too."[4] With her free time, Didrikson often hit golf balls. She had found true passion in the game of golf, and she was eager to return to it.

That's a Gimme

Unlike other sports, the objective of golf is to earn the lowest score, which is the number of times the ball is hit. Like other sports, golf has its own terminology. Unofficial terms such as mulligan (a do-over) and a gimme (a putt that is certain to be made and is conceded by the player's opponent) may be used by casual players but not by the pros. Terms used by all players include:

Front nine: The first nine holes of an 18-hole golf course.

Back nine: The last nine holes of an 18-hole golf course.

Fairway: The well-maintained area within boundaries.

Hole: The ultimate target for the golf ball.

Par: The number of golf strokes considered standard for that hole.

Birdie: Sinking the ball in one stroke less than par for a hole.

Bogey: Sinking the ball in one stroke more than par for that hole.

Hazard: Often water or sand designed to make the play more challenging.

Negative Media Attention

Didrikson had been the golden girl of the Olympics, and now she played a sport against men to earn money. This was highlighted in the media and used as a way to criticize all of women's sports. Although she still enjoyed a comfortable income from her exhibition and promotional work, Didrikson no longer garnered the same respect she had as an Olympian several years prior. Many reporters made negative comments about her short hair and muscular body. One sportswriter, Paul Gallico, famously said that women should only play sports that allowed them to remain looking beautiful. Of sports such as basketball and baseball, he wrote, "A girl just can't do those things and still be a lady."[5] For parents who did not want their sports-oriented daughters to grow up as tomboys, Didrikson represented all that was negative.

Her next endeavor would be golf, a game for the social elite. Not only did her athletic image not fit into traditional feminine stereotypes, her working-class upbringing did not sit well with women in golf at the time. Didrikson was not one to back away from a challenge, however. Fighting prejudice from multiple angles, she would take on the naysayers and change the world of women's golf forever.

Jackie Mitchell, Bob Shafer, and Didrikson were part of an exhibition basketball team that was named Babe Didrikson's All Americans.

CHAPTER 6

Golf instructor Stan Kertes taught Didrikson the game.

A Return to Texas

Having completed her obligations with the All Americans basketball team and the House of David baseball team in the fall of 1934, Babe Didrikson returned to the place she knew she was always welcome: Employers Casualty Company. Although she was back to her old administrative duties, she knew she was destined for something greater.

Didrikson's time spent in Los Angeles with golf professional Stan Kertes planted a seed in her mind. When she signed back on with Employers Casualty, the company's president bought her a membership in the Dallas Country Club to support her newest athletic endeavor. If there was ever an athlete to take a chance on, it was Babe Didrikson.

After taking lessons from George Aulbach, the club professional, Didrikson was ready to showcase her talent. She signed up for the Fort Worth Women's Invitational in November 1934. Going into the qualifying round, Didrikson told a reporter, "I think I'll shoot a seventy-seven."[1]

A Style of Her Own

Didrikson was recognized not for her grace in the game of golf but for her power. After training with Gene Sarazen, she could hit drives as long as 300 yards (274 m) and was more powerful than any other woman golfer.

Although this was quite a goal for someone entering her first golf tournament, she scored exactly what she predicted: 77. Despite being eliminated in an early round, she was encouraged by her performance. With the media following her, she returned to Dallas with a newfound vigor for training. Her next tournament would be the Texas Women's Amateur Championship in the spring of 1935.

Social Class Prejudice

Twenty-three-year-old Didrikson practiced hard for months. Her performance at her first tournament made her a legitimate contender in the state championship. Still, her entry into the competition was questioned. Since she came from a working-class family, many considered that she was not of the proper social class to be involved in the sport of golf, which was dominated by the social elite. One of the premier female golfers at the time, Peggy Chandler, complained, "We really don't need any truck drivers' daughters in this tournament."[2] Nevertheless, the officials were forced to follow the rules. As a member of the Beaumont and Dallas Country Clubs, Didrikson was qualified to enter the tournament.

Despite the underhanded attempts to bar her from competition, Didrikson entered the tournament with

A New Image

Although few of golf's elite were accepting of her, Bertha and R.L. Bowen, who were prominent in Texas golf circles, welcomed and befriended her. Bertha helped Didrikson make a legal appeal to reinstate her amateur status—to no avail.

Although she could not change the ruling, Bertha Bowen was in charge of the Fort Worth Women's Invitational. Using her considerable influence, the event was changed to the Texas Women's Open, which allowed both amateur and professional women golfers. This gave Didrikson one more chance to compete on the mostly amateur golf circuit. Amidst criticism, the Bowens took Didrikson into their home during the tournament and formed a bond. Bertha was instrumental in getting Didrikson accepted in the golf community. Not only did she take Didrikson under her wing and defend her, she also assisted in transforming her image. Bertha encouraged Didrikson to shed her former image to better fit into the social circles in which she now found herself. Otherwise, she feared that Didrikson would find it difficult to get ahead in the game of golf.

her usual ease and confidence. Among 32 other women who qualified, she won her first three rounds, leading her to the semifinals, which she also won. She was on top of her game. The Associated Press proclaimed that she was "still America's wonder girl athlete and probably the most promising woman golf player in the United States."[3] Babe Didrikson was back.

Moving Up the Ranks

In an ironic twist of fate, the final round of the Texas Women's Amateur Championship pitted Didrikson against the woman who had so vocally criticized her. Peggy Chandler was a former state champion and high in the social hierarchy. This was Didrikson's chance to prove that social class had nothing to do with athletic ability. The two women faced each other through 36 grueling holes.

Didrikson gained a comfortable five-up lead over Chandler by the twelfth hole, only to make a string of mistakes at subsequent holes. By the eighteenth hole, Chandler was one up. By the twenty-fourth hole, Chandler was three up. With Chandler's formidable lead so late in the match, Didrikson staged a rally, and the two women were even by the thirty-third hole. On the thirty-fourth hole, a 250-yard (228.6-m) drive by Didrikson ended up in a ditch. In her attempt to hit it out, the ball landed in a wheel rut on a muddy road along the course. To make matters worse, the rut was filled with water from rain the previous day. Both women had taken two shots. With her ball in a puddle, and Chandler's ball on the green, Didrikson's fate appeared to be sealed.

Yet, Didrikson strode confidently to the wheel rut where her ball had landed. Unshaken by the many watchful eyes of the anxious crowd, she selected her sand wedge, inspected the angle, and swung. With that, her ball flew toward the green in a splash of mud and rainwater. The ball bounced onto the green, rolled, and fell into the cup. Onlookers exploded with applause and rushed Didrikson to congratulate her. In the flurry of excitement, her eager fans knocked her into the mud. That shot on the thirty-fourth hole put Didrikson one up, a

Driving Contest

The first shot each player makes on each hole is called a drive or a tee shot. The player's ball is elevated on a wooden tee. The golfer's intent is to drive (hit) the ball the longest distance possible that is suitable for the layout and distance to the green and the hole.

The day before the Texas Women's Amateur Championship began, Didrikson entered a driving contest on the course where the tournament was to be played. A number of the other women subsequently withdrew in protest, suggesting that she was too working class and not feminine enough to be involved in the sport. Didrikson took it in stride, jokingly taking a lazy first swing in the driving contest, parodying the less-powerful swing many expected from a woman. Her next swing was strong and confident, and she launched the ball 300 yards (274 m) to win the contest.

lead she carried through the next two holes to win the tournament.

Turning Pro

Even a state tournament trophy was not enough to convince the United States Golf Association (USGA) that Didrikson belonged in the sport. Following the tournament, the USGA ruled that she could no longer play as an amateur because of her professional status in billiards, baseball, and basketball. Although Didrikson had never made any promotional appearances or received compensation for golf, the USGA declared that her professional involvement in other sports barred her from playing in amateur golf tournaments.

Her supporters fought hard against the ruling, suggesting that it was driven by the USGA's desire to push the girl with the working-class background out of their sophisticated sport. This posed a major problem for Didrikson. At the time, there was only one professional tournament for women: the Western Open. She would not be allowed to play in any of the other tournaments because she was no longer considered an amateur.

Instead of being hindered by the USGA's ruling, Didrikson embraced her professional standing. She traveled the country playing exhibition games with some of the nation's best male golfers and endorsed golf equipment, which allowed her to earn a lucrative income. It was an eerily similar repeat of her first round as a professional athlete when the AAU threatened her amateur status after the Olympics. The line that separated amateur and professional status in women's sports was hazy, and Didrikson continued to be in the crosshairs of the debate.

A New Image

As Didrikson became more immersed in the game of golf and her role as a professional, she also began changing her image. Understanding the importance of fitting in with the golf community, she made visible changes to her wardrobe and appearance. Reporter Paul Gallico commented on her transformation,

Mellowing

In response to the writers who commented on her change in appearance, Didrikson said, "Their idea is that I used to be all tomboy, with none of the usual girls' interests, and then all of a sudden I switched over to being feminine . . . . But I don't believe my personality has changed. I think anyone who knew me when I was a kid will tell you that I'm still the same Babe. It's just that as you get older, you're not as rambunctious as you used to be. You mellow down a little bit."[4]

I hardly knew Babe Didrikson when I saw her. Hair frizzed and she had a neat little wave in it, parted and prettily combed, a touch of rouge on her cheeks and red on her lips. The tomboy had suddenly grown up.[5]

She insisted that she was still the same Babe. However, she felt she needed to look the part of a businesswoman because that was what she was now. Babe Didrikson was looking to gain acceptance in the professional world both in golf and business. Only time would tell if this transformation would translate into fewer obstacles.

Didrikson and Peggy Chandler were opponents in the final round of the Texas Women's Amateur Championship in April 1935.

CHAPTER 7

Wedding Bells

While Babe Didrikson's image changed, so did her approach to the game of golf. She was no longer simply an athlete playing for championships but a businesswoman playing for a living. After the transformation in her appearance, the media had buzzed about whether she would get married. Because Didrikson generally expressed distaste for reporters probing her about her personal life, little is known about any romantic endeavors before 1938.

The Los Angeles Open, a major tournament and part of the men's circuit, did not bar women players. In 1938, Didrikson became the first woman to qualify. She was also realistic about the possibility of winning the event and wrote, "I knew I wasn't going to beat the top men pros, but I was still trying to establish myself as the greatest woman golfer."[1]

In January, the 26-year-old Didrikson met George Zaharias at the Los Angeles Open. An ostentatious and imposing figure, Zaharias was

Los Angeles Open

Didrikson had returned to California in 1936 to work on her golf game with Stan Kertes. She brought her sister, Lillie, and her brother, Arthur, as well as her parents, and put them up in a Los Angeles apartment for $27 per month. After two years of training, she was the first woman ever to qualify and play the Los Angeles Open. While there was no official rule against women playing in the tournament, it was technically part of the men's circuit. Didrikson thought it would be a good stage on which to prove her skills by beating some of the male professionals.

a celebrity in his own right, having enjoyed success in the ring as a professional wrestler. He stood six feet (183 cm) tall and weighed 235 pounds (107 kg). Didrikson described him as "husky and black-haired and handsome."[2] Along with the Presbyterian minister C. Pardee Erdman, Didrikson and Zaharias were teamed together to play at the Los Angeles Open.

Although Didrikson's golf game was not up to par during the tournament, she enjoyed the time spent with Zaharias. They took to each other immediately. Both were fond of the media and chatted with reporters, creating photo opportunities and joking with one another. Their relationship began on the golf course.

The Weeping Greek

George Zaharias, born Theodore Vetoyanis, was the

Wrestler George Zaharias, *left*, posed with his brothers, who also wrestled professionally.

son of Greek immigrants. He grew up with his siblings in a small house with dirt floors near the steel town of Pueblo, Colorado. Like Didrikson, he came from a poor family. As a youngster, he earned money with a variety of jobs. He cleaned hats, worked as a shoeshine boy, and worked with his father in a steel mill. He eventually left Pueblo and joined a traveling circus as a roustabout setting up tents and equipment. In Chicago, he saw a sign offering wrestlers one dollar per day to fight.

Not wanting to embarrass his family, he immediately changed his name to George Zaharias and joined the ranks of professional wrestling. On the wrestling circuit, he became known as the Weeping Greek from Cripple Creek.

Wrestling fans loved Zaharias. In a time when wrestling was as much theater as it was sport, he usually played the role of the villain. Audiences were encouraged to root against him, and many came to watch simply to see whether the villain got what he deserved.

He quickly became a star, making more than $100,000 per year in the late 1930s and early 1940s. At times, he made as much as $15,000 for one night's work. He used some of his first earnings to buy his family a home in Colorado. He also helped finance two of his brothers-in-law in setting up their own business and paid for the education of his two younger brothers. A true showman, he was an impressive actor in the ring. He played a villain, but he was a generous man.

A Budding Romance

Following an intense romance, Didrikson and Zaharias announced their engagement on July 22, 1938. Their travel schedules made selecting a wedding date difficult. When their busy schedules took them both to St. Louis, Missouri, they were married by a justice of the peace on December 23, 1938, at the home of a wrestling promoter.

Because of their many professional commitments, the newlyweds had to delay their honeymoon until the following spring. However, they both continued to work throughout the six-month trip to Australia. Zaharias lined up a number of wrestling commitments, and Didrikson played exhibition golf matches throughout the country. On their cruise back to the United States,

Making the Change to Amateur Status

With few opportunities for female professional golfers, Babe Didrikson had second thoughts regarding her professional status.

Here I'd been practicing all the time, and developing this fine golf game, and about all I could do was play exhibition matches. I wasn't getting a chance to show whether I was the best woman player, because I was barred from practically all of the women's tournaments as a professional.[3]

Originally, Didrikson needed to make money to support herself. Now, with her success and Zaharias's business endeavors, the couple had more than $1 million.

Didrikson missed the competition in golf and wanted to play the most talented female golfers in the world once again and establish herself as the best. Her game was not the only thing that had improved since she was last an amateur. Her physical image had changed, making her a more likely candidate to be accepted and embraced by the golf world. However, she could still be abrasive in her language and demeanor.

During her three-year waiting period, Didrikson continued to practice her golf skills in anticipation of her return to amateur status.

they made stops in New Zealand and Hawaii where Didrikson played golf.

Early in their marriage, Zaharias's wrestling career ended as the result of an injury, and he began managing his wife's career full-time. After the trip to Australia, Didrikson began to rethink her future in golf, however. She had become tired of playing exhibition matches since there were only two professional tournaments for female golfers in the United States. In a moment of realization, she wrote, ". . . what I really wanted in golf was to compete and win championships."[4]

With that decision made, Didrikson canceled her professional contracts and endorsements in January 1940. The USGA rulebook stated that a player had to wait three years before being reinstated as an amateur. This marked the beginning of a long, waiting period during which she anticipated her chance to take on the best in amateur golf once again.

Zaharias and Didrikson married on December 23, 1938.

CHAPTER 8

Didrikson took up tennis during her waiting period to be reinstated as an amateur golfer.

Waiting in the Wings

During the three-year waiting period to regain her amateur status, Babe Didrikson continued to practice her golf game. Although she could not accept any prize money, she won the Women's Western Open and the Texas Women's Open in 1940. These were the only two golf tournaments that she was allowed to enter until she was reinstated as an amateur.

She sought other outlets to fulfill her need to compete during that time. First, she enrolled in tennis lessons at the Beverly Hills Country Club in hopes of learning the game. She once said, "I wanted to see if I could work my way to the top in one more sport."[1] Soon after beginning her lessons and adopting the same tireless approach that she had taken with golf, she was able to beat her instructor, Eleanor Tennant, a longtime professional. Didrikson took on a number of other professionals and beat them as well.

Didrikson gained a reputation as a powerful tennis player. Some claimed she could hit the ball so hard it would pierce the net. Playing 16 sets a day, she trained the same way she did for golf. She practiced so much that a pair of socks lasted only a day on the courts, and her tennis shoes wore out quickly.

After a year and a half of training, Tennant suggested Didrikson enter her first tennis tournament. With great expectations, Didrikson sent her entry to the Pacific Southwest Championships. To her surprise, the tournament's sponsor, the United States Lawn Tennis Association (USLTA), promptly rejected her entry. They informed her that since she had been a professional in other sports, she would never be allowed to compete in tennis at the amateur level. Disappointed that she could not play competitively, she quit playing tennis altogether.

Following her disenchantment with tennis, Didrikson stumbled upon bowling. This sport was governed by different rules that allowed her to play as an amateur. Her introduction to bowling occurred somewhat accidentally. With the popularity of bowling increasing in the United States, Didrikson and Zaharias considered investing in a bowling alley as a business

Rejected

The USLTA's decision disappointed Didrikson: "Once I knew I could never compete in tournaments, that took the fun out of tennis for me. It's not enough for me just to play the game. I have to be able to try for championships. So I quit tennis cold. I still have my rackets, but I haven't touched them from that day to this."[2]

venture. They toured a number of facilities before they decided against purchasing one. In the process, however, Didrikson became intrigued by the game.

She immediately immersed herself in bowling, spending countless hours at the local alleys. She learned from local professionals and bowled for a number of teams in the Los Angeles area. After bowling regularly for a season with the King's Jewelry team of the Southern California Major League, Didrikson's average was a remarkable 170. Not surprisingly, a sports reporter once suggested that Didrikson was "one of the best women bowlers in Southern California."[3]

Wartime Efforts

Throughout her short-lived tennis and bowling careers, Didrikson continued to practice golf. As she waited to be reinstated, Germany's invasion of Poland in 1939 marked the onset of World War II. On December 8, 1941, the United States issued its declaration of war against Germany's ally Japan for the bombing of Pearl Harbor, Hawaii, on December 7. Taking a backseat to the war effort, much of the nation's organized athletic competitions were suspended in the United States.

Didrikson and Zaharias contributed to the war effort by using their involvement in athletics to benefit the troops. Zaharias set up a number of wrestling exhibitions to entertain troops throughout the world. Didrikson played exhibition golf matches to raise money for military charities and sell war bonds.

Didrikson also honed her golf game, waiting for her ban from amateur golf to be lifted. Still, the void left by competitive golf remained. Didrikson was eager to win golf tournaments but also wanted to make the game accessible to more than just men and those of the upper class.

Celebrity Matches

Bob Hope and Bing Crosby were among the most famous celebrities with whom Didrikson played. Hope was a well-known comedian and actor who worked in vaudeville, radio, television, movies, and on stage. He was recognized as a humanitarian and a major supporter of the US armed forces during World War II, the Korean War, the war in Vietnam, and the Persian Gulf War. He was also known for his interest in golf, playing many exhibition tournaments and matches similar to the one he played with Didrikson. He commented, "There's only one thing wrong about Babe and myself. I hit the ball like a girl and she hits it like a man."[4]

Bing Crosby was the third member of Didrikson's comedic golf matches during the war. Crosby was one of the most popular singers of all time, selling over half a billion records. He also branched into film, starring in classic movies, including *White Christmas*. In 1944, he won an Academy Award for Best Actor for *Going My Way*. He was the first to receive the Grammy Lifetime Achievement Award (1962).

Bing Crosby, Didrikson, and Bob Hope played in a celebrity tournament.

CHAPTER 9

Dorothy Germain lost the Women's Western Open golf tournament to Didrikson.

New Beginnings

January 21, 1943, marked Didrikson's long-awaited independence day. She was free to compete as an amateur again. World War II, however, had tempered the excitement for the arrival of that day. As a result of the war, many of the amateur golf tournaments continued to be canceled for the year. While US warplanes dropped bombs overseas, golf seemed of little importance.

Didrikson spent this time playing in various charity tournaments as well as volunteering with children's sports programs. By the summer of 1944, the Women's Western Open gave Didrikson a platform on which to compete as an amateur. She traveled to Indianapolis, Indiana, for the tournament, which she had won as a professional in 1940. She handily won the 1944 title and returned again in 1945, hoping to be the first woman to capture three separate championships.

Heartbreak at Home

Considered a favorite to take the title, Didrikson won her first match at the 1945 Women's Western Open. Advancing to the next round, she received a phone call from her husband with bad news. Her mother had suffered a heart attack and was gravely ill in the hospital. Didrikson frantically tried to get transportation from Indianapolis to Los Angeles to be with her mother. As a result of the war, transportation

Professional Women's Golf Organization

In 1944, a small group of talented women golfers started the Women's Professional Golf Association (WPGA). On shaky financial ground from the start, it lasted until 1948. In May 1948, several players decided to try again to form a professional women's golf tour. Fred Corcoran, Didrikson's agent and sports promoter, was named tournament manager for the new tour.

In August 1950, a group of women players met in Chicago. A few weeks later, the Ladies Professional Golf Association (LPGA) began with 13 founding members, including Didrikson.

In its first year, the LPGA Tour boasted a 14-event schedule with nearly $50,000 in prize money. Didrikson drew crowds with her athleticism, charisma, and one-liners. In her first year on the tour, she dominated the LPGA, winning all three major championships.

By 1959, the LPGA tour had grown to 26 tournaments and $200,000 in prize money. The LPGA is one of the longest-running women's professional sports associations in the world. In 2010, the 27 LPGA tournaments totaled more than $42 million in prize money.

was in a constant state of gridlock. Due to gasoline rationing, American troops were given priority on the limited transport options. Stuck in Indianapolis, and urged on by her husband and sister, she continued to play in the quarterfinals and semifinals. The following day, Didrikson received word that her mother had died. Again, she pushed to get transportation back to Los Angeles and, again, found it to be impossible.

On the verge of tears for much of the last round against Dorothy Germain, Didrikson thought of her mother. She was playing for her now. After shooting 72 in the morning round, she proceeded to make history by winning her third Women's Western Open. She was finally able to fly home for her mother's funeral. It was June 26, 1945, her thirty-fourth birthday.

Amateur Golf Returns

In 1946, the tournament golf schedule was back to what it had been before World War II. Americans looked forward to prosperity and a return to normalcy. Sports were a large part of this movement, and Didrikson was at the forefront.

From August 1946 to the middle of 1947, she had an incredible winning streak of 15 tournaments that was unmatched by any golfer. The previous record was 11 straight tournaments wins by Byron Nelson. Yet her most prestigious win—the 1947 Ladies

British Amateur Championship—was still to come. Although the tournament was first conducted in 1893, no American had ever won it. As she went into the tournament, Didrikson intended to change that.

With incredible momentum from her consecutive wins, Didrikson entered the tournament with confidence. When she arrived in Gullane, Scotland, outside of Edinburgh, she was greeted by many admirers. Her far-reaching fame brought many spectators to the tournament to watch Didrikson and 98 other women compete for the illustrious championship. Each competitor played two 18-hole matches a day. When a golfer lost a match, the player was eliminated from the tournament. When a golfer won, the player advanced. By Thursday, only two women would remain in the competition and play 36 holes for the championship.

The tournament began, and large crowds were drawn to

The Limelight

Few players doubted Didrikson's athletic ability, but she sought the limelight—often in an abrasive and boastful manner. As she walked into the locker room before a golf match, she was known to announce her presence and ask who was going to finish in second place.

Her sense of self-importance was clear when she said, "Let me tell you girls something: you know when there's a star, like in show business, the star has her name in lights on the marquee? Right? And the star gets the money because the people come to see the star, right? Well, I'm the star and all of you are in the chorus. I get the money and if it weren't for me, half of our tournaments wouldn't even be."[1]

watch Didrikson. However, they were far more reserved than golf fans in the United States. This was unsettling to her. After she won her first match she said, "I wish these people would just holler and enjoy themselves the way the crowds do back home."[2] A true performer, she began chatting with the crowds and encouraging them to make noise after she hit.

By the end of the second match on Monday, Didrikson won over the crowds. After she clinched the match win by the sixteenth hole, she suggested to her opponent that they play the seventeenth and eighteenth holes even though it would not change the outcome of the match. This was a common practice in the United States but not in Scotland. As she performed several of her trick shots, the entire gallery roared with applause. In the most crowd-pleasing shot, she placed a match behind her ball and swung mightily for one of her signature 250-yard (229-m) drives. As the head of the club came through, it struck the match and with a loud pop, lit the flame, simultaneously sending the ball rocketing off into the distance. By the end of the tournament, Didrikson's gallery swelled to more than 8,000 spectators. She was quite different than the Scots, and they loved her.

Didrikson continued to advance throughout the week, winning in the semifinals and advancing to the finals against renowned British golfer Jacqueline

Generosity

Unprepared for Scotland's unpredictably cool weather, Didrikson mentioned her discomfort to reporters during the Ladies British Amateur. Soon after stories ran, generous Scots flooded her hotel with donations of warm clothes. She received so many bundles of clothing they spilled out of her room and were stacked in the hotel hallways and lobby. From the piles, she chose a World War II jumpsuit and corduroy pants to take with her on the course and slip on when the temperature dropped. The corduroy pants would come to be called her "lucky pants."

Gordon. After the morning round of 18 holes, Didrikson and Gordon were dead even. She knew she was not playing her best.

Didrikson had not packed clothing for the cold weather, but a number of local Scots had donated warm clothes. She liked a pair of corduroy pants in particular. Urged on by the crowd who believed the pants to be good luck, Didrikson fetched them before the next round. Donning her lucky pants for the second round of the day, she won the first of 18 holes. Her luck continued after that. After the thirty-second hole, she was five up, with just four holes to go. Spectators erupted in thunderous applause. Babe Didrikson Zaharias became the first American to win the Ladies British Amateur Championship. Her winning streak remained intact.

Didrikson held up the trophy after winning the Ladies British
Amateur Championship.

The Lure of Professional Golf

Upon returning home from Scotland, Didrikson's fame was at an all-time high. The Associated Press sports editors' poll named her the Female Athlete of the Year for a fourth time in 1947. Not only had she become the greatest female golfer the world had ever known, she also became a celebrity. Eventually, she could no longer resist the many big endorsement deals that were offered to her. After the long struggle to achieve amateur status, Didrikson made the difficult decision to become a professional once again. Earning more than $100,000 per year, she traveled the country playing exhibition games and making special appearances.

Didrikson had a strong desire for competition. With few opportunities for

"Babe changed the game of golf for women—not only by bringing along the LPGA, but by her kind of golf. She came along with that great power game and it led to lower scores and more excitement . . . and she brought all that humor and showman-ship to the game. She humanized it. She was the happiest girl you ever saw, like a kid. Our sport grew because of Babe, because she had so much flair and color."[3]
—*Patty Berg, professional golfer and first president of the LPGA*

Didrikson signed a contract to become a professional golfer as her husband, George Zaharias, and Fred Corcoran of the Professional Golfers Association (PGA) watched.

professional female golfers, she set out to influence changes in the sport. She wanted to create an organization that would allow women to make a living playing competitive golf. Fred Corcoran helped her get a charter drawn up for the newly formed Ladies Professional Golf Association (LPGA). In years to come, the organization would attract the country's best female golfers.

As the LPGA developed, Didrikson continued to redefine the sport. In 1950, she won six professional tournaments, including the Women's All-American tournament at Chicago's Tam O'Shanter Country Club in August. She also won more prize money than anyone else that year. With endorsements and prize winnings, her agent claimed that Babe Didrikson was the first female athlete to earn six figures. By the end of that year, she was named the AP's Female Athlete of the Year and the Half Century. After winning another seven LPGA tournaments in 1951, it seemed as if nothing could stop her. Unfortunately, life sometimes takes unexpected turns.

Didrikson on the eighteenth green at the Tam O'Shanter Country Club in the Women's All-American Golf Tournament

CHAPTER 10

Betty Dodd played the guitar and Didrikson played the harmonica.

Fighting the Odds

While Babe Didrikson's worldwide fame blossomed, her marriage with Zaharias became strained. While he tirelessly promoted his wife's athletic endeavors, he missed the fame and attention he had experienced as a professional wrestler. His eating habits became a constant issue between the couple. A strong and imposing figure when they first met, his weight had soared to more than 400 pounds (182 kg). His appearance, appetite, and table manners strained their marriage. Arguments were sparked by his massive consumption of food as he would eat sticks of butter and excessively soak pieces of bread in olive oil. He was angry, feeling that he had lost control of her professional life as she made more decisions independently. Despite their disagreements, the couple always appeared happy under the media's watchful eye.

Although Didrikson became lonely in her marriage, she found companionship in a close friend, Betty Dodd. The two women met in Miami,

Florida, in 1950 at a golf tournament and discovered they had much in common. Dodd was 20 years younger than Didrikson, who was at the apex of her career. She became Didrikson's protégé, traveling to tournaments around the country and playing alongside her. Dodd loved playing the guitar, and Didrikson continued to practice the harmonica. The duo entertained other players at tournaments as they showcased their musical talents. Eventually, Dodd moved in with Didrikson and Zaharias in their Florida home. Although a houseguest at first, she later played an integral role in helping Didrikson overcome the biggest challenge she had ever faced.

Babe's Highest Hurdle

A jam-packed tournament schedule kicked off Didrikson's 1952 season. Along with a number of exhibition games and an appearance in the latest Katharine Hepburn movie, *Pat and Mike*, she was on top of the golf world. Following a routine surgery for a strangulated hernia in her thigh, she spent a short time recovering at her home in Tampa, Florida. She was back on the golf course by the end of the summer but was constantly tired and had difficulty finishing a full round of 18 holes.

After a short break that allowed Didrikson time to rest after the season, she returned to the circuit at the beginning of 1953. Her fatigue continued and affected her playing abilities. No longer could she assume a long string of victories, and she won only one tournament in the spring. Upon the insistence of Dodd and Zaharias, Didrikson visited her doctor, W. E. Tatum.

The news was not good. Tatum discovered a malignancy in Didrikson's lower intestine and diagnosed colon cancer. She had seen her father die of cancer and was frightened. Her only option was a serious operation, called a colostomy, which would be physically devastating to the long-time athlete. The tumor would be removed by cutting off a piece of her lower intestine and connecting part of the colon onto the abdomen wall. The intestinal tract would be rerouted to pass solid waste through an incision, called a stoma, in the abdomen. Didrikson's doctor reported to the Associated Press, "I don't know yet if surgery will cure her, but I will say that she never again will play golf of championship caliber."[1]

The team of doctors successfully performed the colostomy on April 17, 1953. However, during surgery, they found that the cancer had

A Competitor

After her surgery, Didrikson wrote, "All my life I've been competing—and competing to win. I came to realize that in its way, this cancer was the toughest competition I'd faced yet. I made up my mind that I was going to lick it all the way . . . I was determined to come back and win golf championships just the same as before."[2]

spread to Didrikson's lymph nodes and was inoperable. This diagnosis meant that the golf great was sure to encounter more health problems in the near future. As was common practice in the 1950s, her doctor suggested that the information be kept from her. Zaharias and Dodd agreed that it would only dash her spirits and hinder the recovery process.

The Road to Recovery

Encouraged by an outpouring of thousands of letters and telegrams from fans, Didrikson quickly began to feel better. Just ten days after surgery, she was pacing the hospital hallways and socializing with other patients. Soon she began doing strength exercises and practicing her swing in her hospital room. Despite doubts from the media and her doctors, she knew she would return to golf. She had beaten the odds before, and she intended to do it again.

Fourteen weeks after her colostomy, Didrikson tried her hand at the All-American Tournament at the Tam O'Shanter Country Club in Illinois. Worried about putting stress on her intestinal tract, Didrikson asked to be paired with Dodd during the tournament. Dodd had been with her through every step of the recovery process and was the only person who knew how to help her if needed. Dodd had become Didrikson's caretaker and companion.

While swinging a club was a feat in itself, Didrikson found her golf game to be nothing close to what it had been before. After the third round, in a private moment with Dodd, she broke down in defeat. Considering Didrikson's pain, fatigue, and colostomy bag, Dodd suggested that no one would blame her for quitting. Didrikson retorted earnestly, "No, no. I don't want to quit. I'm not a quitter."[3] She pressed on, finishing in a disappointing fifteenth place.

Speaking Up

Always generous with her time and money, Babe Didrikson gave a public face to cancer victims everywhere. She was one of the first high-profile individuals to speak publicly about the disease. In 1954, after her inspiring post-cancer comeback, she was invited to the White House to help kick off the American Cancer Society's annual fund-raising drive with President Dwight Eisenhower. Fund-raising throughout the country benefited from having her as a spokesperson.

Even though she had signs of the cancer returning, she worked hard to raise money for cancer awareness and research.

In 1955, she opened the Babe Didrikson Zaharias chapter of the American Cancer Society in Seattle, Washington. Soon afterward, she and her husband announced the Babe Didrikson Zaharias Cancer Fund. She continued to play on the golf tour in 1955 and visited area hospitals where her tournaments were held. She met with other cancer patients and worked to ease their emotional pain. Sometimes, she and Betty Dodd put on a show with the harmonica and guitar. Didrikson brought cancer out into the limelight, encouraging people to talk about a disease that deserved attention.

The Comeback

Didrikson was no quitter. After the All-American Tournament, she went on to finish third at the World Golf Championship as well as finishing as the sixth-highest money winner for the season. She was awarded the Ben Hogan Comeback of the Year Award for her resiliency and strength in the face of incredible obstacles.

Although she got off to a slow start during the 1954 season, she eventually began to show glimmers of the Babe Didrikson everyone remembered before the cancer. She won five tournaments, including the 1954 Serbin Open, which marked her first win after surgery for cancer. She was named the Female Athlete of the Year by the Associated Press for a sixth time over a period of 22 years. Didrikson proved the impossible to be possible. Those who claimed she would never play again were wrong. It seemed that she had faced her cancer and triumphed. These victories, however, were only in the short term. The year 1954 would be her last shining season on the golf course.

A Mighty Champion

Didrikson began the 1955 season by winning the Tampa Women's Open and the Peach Blossom Open. Shortly thereafter, Didrikson began experiencing back pains. In the beginning, she played through the pain

Didrikson won the 1954 Serbin Open—her first win after cancer surgery.

and endured the discomfort. Eventually, she visited her doctor. As she feared, the cancer had returned.

While Zaharias and Dodd had known it was only a matter of time, Didrikson was unaware that she had never been completely cancer free. The cancer had spread to her lower spine, and doctors were unable to operate in that area. By October 1955, Didrikson's pain increased. As she fought the cancer, she took to working on her autobiography. She also enjoyed a visit from her former golf competitor, Peggy Kirk Bell. Due to Didrikson's physical deterioration, even putting her golf shoes on was impossible. Nevertheless, she insisted on playing a round of golf with Bell. Wearing loafers, she played a relaxed game, though both she and Bell knew that the cancer was taking Didrikson one day at a time. This was the last round the golf legend played.

Another Diagnosis

Zaharias faced reporters following his wife's latest diagnosis, saying, "[Babe] took the bad news like the mighty champion she has always been. . . . She's not giving up . . . she never flinched when told she had another cancer."[4]

In and out of the hospital, Didrikson worked on her autobiography, but she was unable to perform even menial physical tasks any longer. On December 26, she asked to be driven to the local golf course. As she slowly and painfully walked out to the eighteenth green, she no doubt thought of her many victories in a game that had so defined her life. She knelt down and touched the impeccably groomed, soft grass. She explained sadly, "I just wanted to see a golf course one more time."[5] Babe Didrikson knew she was nearing the end of her life and was beginning to say good-bye.

Never Quit

The deterioration of her physical state was long and painful. In March 1956, Didrikson entered the hospital once again. As she lay in her bed at the John Sealy Hospital in Galveston, Texas, she continued to receive many letters from adoring fans. Dodd went back on the golf tour upon the urging of Didrikson. Zaharias remained with his wife, serving as a tearful spokesperson for her in press conferences.

In the early hours of the morning on September 27, 1956, after three years of fighting cancer, Babe Didrikson Zaharias died in the hospital. She was 45 years old. She had kept her golf clubs in the corner of the hospital room, never completely giving up on the sport she loved. Zaharias's death made front-page news throughout the country. A *New York Times* reporter wrote,

> She didn't know the meaning of the word quit, and she refused to define it, right to the end. It is not only the annals of sport that her life has enriched. It is the whole story of human beings who somehow have to keep trying.[6]

The spirited child of poor Norwegian immigrants had found her way into the hearts and minds of sports fans everywhere. First she achieved Olympic gold, then stardom. Her golden years in golf were her best. Didrikson left behind an athletic legacy, but more importantly, she is remembered for her ability to overcome tremendous odds and prove the world wrong when they did not believe in her. In the end, the doubters were few. Whether the hurdles were hedges on Doucette Avenue, public scrutiny, or a deadly cancer, Babe Didrikson, a figure of legendary proportions, approached each with determination and resolve.

A President's Tribute

On the morning of Didrikson's death, President Dwight Eisenhower made a heartfelt announcement: "Ladies and gentlemen, I should like to take one minute to pay a tribute to Mrs. Zaharias, Babe Didrikson. She was a woman who in her athletic career certainly won the admiration of every person in the United States, all sports people over the world. I think every one of us feels sad that finally she had to lose this last one of all her battles."[7]

At a cancer crusade event, Didrikson gave President Eisenhower some tips on golf grips.

1911

Mildred Ella "Babe" Didriksen is born in Texas on June 26.

1915

A hurricane hits the Didriksen home in Port Arthur, Texas. The family moves to Beaumont, Texas.

1930

Colonel Melvin Jackson McCombs offers Didrikson a job and a spot on the Golden Cyclones basketball team.

1932

On July 18, the US Olympic women's track and field team travels to Los Angeles for the 1932 Summer Olympic Games.

1932

Didrikson returns home from the Olympics on August 11 and is greeted by 10,000 people.

1934

Didrikson enters her first golf tournament, the Fort Worth Women's Invitational, in November.

1930

Didrikson arrives in Dallas and plays in her first amateur basketball game for the Golden Cyclones on February 18.

1930

In late spring, Didrikson enters her first track meet at Southern Methodist University. She wins four events.

1932

Didrikson enters the US Olympic Trials for track and field, earning a spot on the 1932 US Olympic team.

1938

Didrikson meets George Zaharias at the Los Angeles Open in January.

1938

Didrikson and Zaharias announce their engagement on July 22.

1938

Didrikson and Zaharias marry in St. Louis, Missouri, on December 23.

TIMELINE

1940

In January, Didrikson cancels her professional golf contract and begins a three-year waiting period to be considered an amateur again.

1943

Didrikson's amateur standing with the USGA is restored on January 21.

1946

Didrikson begins a winning streak of 17 consecutive tournaments.

1953

On April 17, surgeons perform a colostomy on Didrikson in hopes of curing her colon cancer.

1953

Didrikson returns to golf for the All-American Tournament at the Tam O'Shanter Country Club on July 31.

1953

Didrikson is awarded the Ben Hogan Comeback of the Year Award.

1947

1947

1950

In June, Didrikson wins the Ladies British Amateur Championship in Scotland.

Didrikson is a cofounder of the Ladies Professional Golf Association (LPGA).

Didrikson is named the Female Athlete of the Half Century.

1954

1955

1956

Didrikson wins the Serbin Open, her first win after cancer surgery.

Didrikson publishes her autobiography, *This Life I've Led*.

On September 27, Didrikson dies of cancer in Galveston, Texas, at the age of 45.

DATE OF BIRTH
June 26, 1911

PLACE OF BIRTH
Port Arthur, Texas

DATE OF DEATH
September 27, 1956

PARENTS
Ole Nickolene Didriksen and Hannah Marie Olson Didriksen

EDUCATION
During her senior year, and with the approval of her parents, 18-year-old Babe accepted a job with Employers Casualty in Dallas, Texas, to play basketball for the company's team called the Golden Cyclones. She was allowed to return to her school at the end of the year to take her final exams and graduate from high school.

MARRIAGE
George Zaharias (December 23, 1938)

CHILDREN
None

CAREER HIGHLIGHTS

Babe Didrikson made headlines when she won the team title at the 1932 AAU National Championship track and field meet on her own, competing in eight of the ten events. The victory qualified her for the 1932 Olympic Games. She emerged from those games with two gold medals and one silver medal. Her greatest victories, however, occurred in the game of golf. She was the first American woman to win the British Amateur Championship. She also won three US Women's Open Championships and 55 tournaments overall.

SOCIETAL CONTRIBUTIONS

Along with her personal triumphs, Didrikson helped to found the Ladies Professional Golf Association (LPGA) in 1950 and advance women's sports. She and her husband, George Zaharias, established the Babe Zaharias Cancer Fund to support cancer clinics.

CONFLICTS

Didrikson was twice ensnared in conflict with the Amateur Athletic Union regarding her status in sports. This led to Didrikson's switching back and forth between professional and amateur roles, which challenged her to decide between money and competition. In addition, Didrikson was regularly criticized by the media for her atypical projection of femininity. Along with fighting sexism, she encountered prejudice as a woman from a working-class family entering into the world of golf, a game for the social elite.

QUOTE

"Before I was ever in my teens, I knew exactly what I wanted to be when I grew up. My goal was to be the greatest athlete that ever lived." —*Babe Didrikson*

GLOSSARY

agent
>A person who is authorized to act on someone's behalf in business negotiations.

apex
>The highest point.

barnstorm
>To travel around rural areas putting on performances.

billiards
>A two-person game played on a billiards table in which balls are hit with cue sticks into pockets affixed to the table.

cartilage
>A type of connective tissue in the body.

chaotic
>In a state of confusion.

compensation
>Payment for work or endorsement of a product.

formidable
>Inspiring respect or fear due to great size, power, or capacity.

gallery
>Spectators at a golfing event.

Great Depression
>A period of worldwide economic hardship from 1929 until the early 1940s that began in the United States with the 1929 stock market crash.

heptathlon
>A seven-event track and field competition.

javelin
A slender wood or metal spear that is thrown for distance in a field event.

naysayer
A person who expresses doubt regarding a person or event.

protégé
A person whose career is furthered by a person of greater experience or influence.

prowess
Extraordinary skill or ability.

rambunctious
Loudly or actively enthusiastic.

technique
The way or style through which a specific task is carried out.

transformation
A striking change in appearance.

tutelage
Being instructed.

unorthodox
Differing from the norm or what is widely accepted.

World War II
A worldwide conflict that occurred between 1939 and 1945 that involved many of the world's nations and more than 100 million military personnel.

ADDITIONAL RESOURCES

SELECTED BIBLIOGRAPHY

Cayleff, Susan E. *Babe: The Life and Legend of Babe Didrikson Zaharias.* Chicago: University of Illinois Press, 1995. Print.

Freedman, Russell. *Babe Didrikson Zaharias: The Making of a Champion.* New York: Clarion Books, 1999. Print.

Johnson, William Oscar, and Nancy P. Williamson. *"Whatta-Gal": The Babe Didrikson Story.* Boston: Little, Brown and Company, 1975. Print.

Zaharias, Babe Didrikson, and Harry Paxton. *This Life I've Led: My Autobiography.* New York: A. S. Barnes and Company, 1955. Print.

FURTHER READINGS

Cayleff, Susan. E. *Babe Didrikson: The Greatest All-Sport Athlete of All Time.* Chicago: University of Illinois Press, 1995.

Hasday, Judy. *Extraordinary Women Athletes (Extraordinary People).* New York: Children's Press, 2000.

Lynn, Elizabeth A. *Babe Didrikson Zaharias.* New York: Chelsea House Publishers, 1989.

Vecchione, Joseph. *New York Times Book of Sports Legends.* New York: Fireside, 1991.

WEB LINKS

To learn more about Babe Didrikson Zaharias, visit ABDO Publishing Company online at **www.abdopublishing.com**. Web sites about Babe Didrikson Zaharias are featured on our Book Links page. These links are routinely monitored and updated to provide the most current information available.

PLACES TO VISIT

The Babe Didrikson Zaharias Museum
1750 E IH-10 Beaumont, TX 77704
409-833-4622
http://www.babedidriksonzaharias.org/museum.cfm
The Babe Didrikson Zaharias Museum is dedicated to the famous golf great and sportswoman. Located in the town in which she grew up, the museum is also the Chamber of Commerce welcoming center for the city.

Forest Lawn Memorial Park and Cemetery
4955 Pine Street Beaumont, TX 77703
409-892-5912
Babe Didrikson's grave site is in Forest Lawn Memorial Park in Beaumont, Texas. Along with her headstone, a plaque is dedicated to her and her many athletic achievements.

World Golf Hall of Fame
One World Golf Place, St. Augustine, FL 32092
904-940-4000
http://www.worldgolfhalloffame.org
Babe Didrikson Zaharias was one of the inductees into the LPGA Tour Hall of Fame in 1951. LPGA Hall of Fame members are now honored at the World Golf Hall of Fame in St. Augustine, Florida. You can learn about the history of golf and try your skills at the hands-on exhibits.

SOURCE NOTES

CHAPTER 1. A One-Woman Show

1. Russell Freedman. *Babe Didrikson Zaharias: The Making of a Champion*. New York: Clarion Books, 1999. Print. 49.

2. Babe Didrikson Zaharias and Harry Paxton. *This Life I've Led: My Autobiography*. New York: Barnes, 1955. Print. 45.

3. Ibid. 50.

4. Ibid.

5. Ibid. 48.

CHAPTER 2. Growing Up in Texas

1. William Oscar Johnson and Nancy P. Williamson. *"Whatta-Gal": The Babe Didrikson Story*. Boston: Little, 1975. Print. 36.

2. Russell Freedman. *Babe Didrikson Zaharias: The Making of a Champion*. New York: Clarion Books, 1999. Print. 19.

3. Babe Didrikson Zaharias and Harry Paxton. *This Life I've Led: My Autobiography*. New York: Barnes, 1955. Print. 25.

4. Susan E. Cayleff. *Babe: The Life and Legend of Babe Didrikson Zaharias*. Chicago: U of Illinois Press, 1995. Print. 34.

5. William Oscar Johnson and Nancy P. Williamson. *"Whatta-Gal": The Babe Didrikson Story*. Boston: Little, 1975. Print. 43.

6. Russell Freedman. *Babe Didrikson Zaharias: The Making of a Champion*. New York: Clarion Books, 1999. Print. 26.

7. Ibid. 9.

CHAPTER 3. National Recognition

1. Susan E Cayleff. *Babe: The Life and Legend of Babe Didrikson Zaharias*. Chicago: U of Illinois Press, 1995. Print. 41.

2. William Oscar Johnson and Nancy P. Williamson. *"Whatta-Gal": The Babe Didrikson Story*. Boston: Little, 1975. Print. 73.

CHAPTER 4. The 1932 Olympics

1. Babe Didrikson Zaharias and Harry Paxton. *This Life I've Led: My Autobiography*. New York: Barnes, 1955. Print. 52.

2. Russell Freedman. *Babe Didrikson Zaharias: The Making of a Champion*. New York: Clarion Books, 1999. Print. 60.

3. William Oscar Johnson and Nancy P. Williamson. *"Whatta-Gal": The Babe Didrikson Story*. Boston: Little, 1975. Print. 6.

4. Ibid. 106.

5. Ibid. 107.

CHAPTER 5. An Unwelcome Scandal

1. William Oscar Johnson and Nancy P. Williamson. *"Whatta-Gal": The Babe Didrikson Story*. Boston: Little, 1975. Print. 4.

2. Ibid. 138.

3. Susan E. Cayleff. *Babe: The Life and Legend of Babe Didrikson Zaharias*. Chicago: U of Illinois Press, 1995. Print. 120.

4. Russell Freedman. *Babe Didrikson Zaharias: The Making of a Champion*. New York: Clarion Books, 1999. Print. 82.

5. Susan E. Cayleff. *Babe: The Life and Legend of Babe Didrikson Zaharias*. Chicago: U of Illinois Press, 1995. Print. 86.

CHAPTER 6. A Return to Texas

1. Babe Didrikson Zaharias and Harry Paxton. *This Life I've Led: My Autobiography*. New York: Barnes, 1955. Print. 87.

2. William Oscar Johnson and Nancy P. Williamson. *"Whatta-Gal": The Babe Didrikson Story*. Boston: Little, 1975. Print. 124.

3. Babe Didrikson Zaharias and Harry Paxton. *This Life I've Led: My Autobiography*. New York: Barnes, 1955. Print. 93.

4. Ibid. 103.

5. William Oscar Johnson and Nancy P. Williamson. *"Whatta-Gal": The Babe Didrikson Story*. Boston: Little, 1975. Print. 153.

CHAPTER 7. Wedding Bells

1. Russell Freedman. *Babe Didrikson Zaharias: The Making of a Champion*. New York: Clarion Books, 1999. Print. 101.
2. Babe Didrikson Zaharias and Harry Paxton. *This Life I've Led: My Autobiography*. New York: Barnes, 1955. Print. 105.
3. Ibid. 119.
4. Ibid. 120.

CHAPTER 8. Waiting in the Wings

1. Babe Didrikson Zaharias and Harry Paxton. *This Life I've Led: My Autobiography*. New York: Barnes, 1955. Print. 122.
2. Ibid. 125.
3. Susan E. Cayleff. *Babe: The Life and Legend of Babe Didrikson Zaharias*. Chicago: U of Illinois Press, 1995. Print. 146.
4. Ibid. 148.

CHAPTER 9. New Beginnings

1. Susan Ware. *Letter to the World. Seven Women Who Shaped the American Century*. New York: Norton, 1998. Print. 199.
2. Babe Didrikson Zaharias and Harry Paxton. *This Life I've Led: My Autobiography*. New York: Barnes, 1955. Print. 162.
3. William Oscar Johnson and Nancy P. Williamson. *"Whatta-Gal": The Babe Didrikson Story*. Boston: Little, 1975. Print. 190.

CHAPTER 10. Fighting the Odds

1. William Oscar Johnson and Nancy P. Williamson. *"Whatta-Gal": The Babe Didrikson Story.* Boston: Little, 1975. Print. 204.

2. Russell Freedman. *Babe Didrikson Zaharias: The Making of a Champion.* New York: Clarion Books, 1999. Print. 154.

3. William Oscar Johnson and Nancy P. Williamson. *"Whatta-Gal": The Babe Didrikson Story.* Boston: Little, 1975. Print. 209.

4. Susan E. Cayleff. *Babe: The Life and Legend of Babe Didrikson Zaharias.* Chicago: U of Illinois Press, 1995. Print. 233.

5. Russell Freedman. *Babe Didrikson Zaharias: The Making of a Champion.* New York: Clarion Books, 1999. Print. 160.

6. Ibid. 163.

7. William Oscar Johnson and Nancy P. Williamson. *"Whatta-Gal": The Babe Didrikson Story.* Boston: Little, 1975. Print. 3.

INDEX

ABOUT THE AUTHOR

Mackenzie Lobby is a freelance writer and editor who has worked on many books for young people. She holds a bachelor's degree in English from the College of St. Benedict/ St. John's University. She has also earned a master's degree in kinesiology with an emphasis in sports psychology from the University of Minnesota. She lives and writes in Minneapolis, Minnesota.

PHOTO CREDITS